Miriam Coots

1994

The Logia of Yeshua

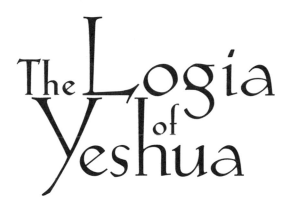

The Logia of Yeshua

The Sayings of Jesus

Translated by

Guy Davenport

and

Benjamin Urrutia

COUNTERPOINT
WASHINGTON, D.C.

Frontispiece: The draught of fishes (medieval woodcut, artist
unidentified); collection of Guy Davenport

Library of Congress Catalog Card Number 96–83236

ISBN 1–887178–18–x

FIRST PRINTING

Book design and production by David Bullen

Printed in the United States of America on acid-free paper that
meets the American National Standards Institute z39–48 Standard.

COUNTERPOINT
P.O. Box 65793
Washington, D.C. 20035–5793
Distributed by Publishers Group West

Contents

Prologue

In the beginning was the Logion.

Logion (plural logia), originally the Greek for "saying," is now a technical term for important sayings of famous men of antiquity, such as Heraclitus, Socrates, and Yeshua, whom we commonly call "Jesus." Collections of Yeshua's logia— "Sayings Gospels"—preceded the now familiar gospels, just as the Yeshua Movement preceded the Christian Church. Among these early collections was a Hebrew document, attributed to Matthew, which may or may not be the same as "Q" (the hypothetical source of logia for both the Gospels of Matthew and of Luke). Another was the Gospel of Thomas, which later was expanded, translated into Coptic, and then expanded some more. Of the multitude of gospels that, according to Luke, preceded his own, at least these two or three, or perhaps a considerable portion, were Sayings Gospels.

Why was there a whole genre of gospels that consisted entirely of logia, without accounts of the Nativity, the Crucifixion, the Resurrection? Let us remember that Mark and John show no interest either in the story of Yeshua's birth. And it is quite possible that to many early followers of Yeshua his death was just as irrelevant as his birth was to Mark's and John's readers. Only what Yeshua taught mattered—not the story of his life. It is also possible—though not too likely—that the first logia collections may have been written *before* the Crucifixion and Resurrection, so they could not be expected to mention them, except, perhaps, prophetically.

If the gospels of the logia were written soon after the Crucifixion, as they probably were, their authors and readers may have felt that they were in no danger of forgetting the tragic and earthshaking events, but the Sayings needed to be written down to be remembered accurately by the community.

For Docetics and Gnostics, who denied the reality of the Crucifixion, the Sayings Gospels proved to be a very congenial genre. Unfortunately, they could not resist adding their own bits of so-called Gnosis to them. Neither were the authors of the "Orthodox" mainstream gospels above glossing the logia (as well as, of course, combining them with accounts of the Crucifixion and Resurrection—and of the Nativity in a couple of cases).

The original logia were shocking and paradoxical, somewhat like Zen koans or Sufi anecdotes. The Orthodox evangelists softened the hard sayings and dulled their sharp edges by covering them up with facile explanations and simplistic morals at the conclusion of subversive parables. Worst of all, many logia were embedded in tendentious stories that served the purposes of the growing churches.

Søren Kierkegaard averred that the churches are the sepulchres of the prophets. Similarly, the gospels are the graves of the logia. Presenting the sayings of Yeshua without the ecclesiastical accretions is akin to what the Wahabbis of Saudi Arabia did when they smashed the tombs of the prophets and saints in their iconoclastic struggle against superstition and idolatry. Here are the logia themselves, freed from glosses and simplistic morals.

I began the compilation and editing in 1977. At a certain stage, I asked Professor Davenport for his opinion. His suggestions, both for the work as a whole and for specific changes, were so valuable that I invited him to collaborate. We made several drafts, each of us revising the other's phrasing, until the text became a true and seamless fusion of our ideas about how the logia should sound in the modern English language.

We have kept commentary to a bare minimum. In the Sources and Notes at the end of this book we give our reasons for our most unorthodox inclusions and idiosyncratic translations. Otherwise, we let the sayings speak for themselves.

For any and all errors, we accept full responsibility, and ask to have them pointed out logically, rationally, and specifically. We also urge readers not to submit to the authority of churches or scholars, but to decide for themselves which of the logia are authentic.

This work is dedicated to Shannon Cole, who assisted the work with praise and encouragement; to Kent Jeppsen, who read parts of several drafts and made valuable suggestions for improvements; and to my friend Gracia Fay Ellwood and my teacher Dr. Hugh Nibley, who have helped me to understand better the life, teachings, and personality of Yeshua.

We are in debt to hundreds of scholars who have studied the life and logia of Yeshua and written and taught about them. The following, listed in alphabetical order, have made specific proposals that we have used:

Harvey Falk, author of *Jesus the Pharisee: A New Look at the Jewishness of Jesus.*

Robert Graves and Joshua Podro, authors of *The Nazarene Gospel Restored.*

The Scholars of the Jesus Seminar.

Stephen Mitchell, author of *The Gospel According to Jesus*.

Geza Vermes, author of *Jesus the Jew: A Historian's Reading of the Gospels*.

BENJAMIN URRUTIA

Introduction

This little book of Jesus' sayings began with a fortuitous encounter. Benjamin Urrutia—teacher, soldier in the Israeli army, writer, linguist, scholar, and Basque Jewish Christian born in South America—read a story of mine in *A Table of Green Fields*, in which he saw that I had used various papyri and Talmudic sources. The story is about the child Jesus (Yeshua, that is, *Joshua*, which gets spelled *Iesous* in Greek and *Jesus* in Latin) one-upping his teacher in school. Benjamin, probably alone among my readers, recognized little Yeshua's "We haven't yet finished with *alef* and here we are going on to *beth*" as an anecdote from an ancient manuscript, *The Stories of Thomas the Israelite, the Philosopher, Concerning the Works of the Childhood of the Lord*. Moreover, the passage out of which I made my story has a phrase muddled by a scribe, which I realized survives in Jewish learning, and I restored it from a commentary by Rabbi Schneur Zalman.

Benjamin thought that the twelve-year-old Yeshua just *might* have said it. It is a quotation and is in character with his habit of weaving scripture and traditional sayings in a large amount of his teaching. So, in Benjamin's translation, we have made it the first *logion*.

One of the first sayings of Yeshua that I learned (my mother quoted it daily) is not in the gospels. "It is better to give than to receive" (Acts 20:35) is a logion known to Paul before the gospels were written. It is a general understanding among scholars that collections of the *logia* were used by the earliest congregations before they had gospels. The Gnostic Gospel of Thomas, for instance (from which we have taken a number of sayings), is all logia and no narrative at all.

Some years ago, while teaching a course in archaic thought (that of Heraclitus and the West African Dogon), I was so dissatisfied with available translations of Heraclitus, all of which were distorted by philosophical theory, that I made my own, a naked translation that baldly duplicated in English what the Greek seemed to say. Any road goes two ways, according to which direction you're going on it. So Heraclitus's saying has all kinds of implications, none of which may have been "The Way up and the Way down are one and the same" (mystical coloring from the Chinese *tao* and a poetic pessimism). I was trying to extricate Heraclitus from several of his interpretations. This translation was passed around, printed here and there in small magazines, and eventually got published by Donald Allen along with the logia of Diogenes (and is now also in my *Seven Greeks*) and has been the best-seller among my modest output. ("Greek bumper stickers" said *The Whole Earth Catalog*.)

When I was translating these logia, it kept occurring to me that Yeshua was, in one sense, a fusion of Heraclitus (for whom there is an ethics to be discovered in nature) and Diogenes, who, like Yeshua, was a street preacher and for whom ethics was a minute-by-minute exercise of moral rectitude.

When I learned from Benjamin Urrutia that he was working on a scholarly book about the logia of Yeshua, I suggested that he also do a little book like my Heraclitus and Diogenes—the sayings each by itself, without theological directing and without their biblical context. Christians of all sorts would know the contexts. We would simply be locating a figure on a ground, lifting it out, and giving it a new chance for recognition and study. We would also make our own translation.

Most Christians know what Yeshua said in the lovely and stately Reformation English of William Tyndale, the most gifted of translators since Jerome (who put the Greek text of the Bible into Latin). Tyndale's translation, and its appropriation by the translators of the 1611 "King James version," is truly hallowed, and any deviation from it makes us uncomfortable.

We do not yet know if Yeshua spoke *koine* (common-market Greek) or Aramaic. The writers of the gospels thought that their best hope for disseminating the Good News was to write in Greek, so a Greek-speaking Yeshua is what the world got.

There is a papyrus fragment of a lost gospel on which only a few sentences are legible. It was written in the first century and is therefore as close to Yeshua's time as the canonical gospels. Yeshua is on the banks of the Jordan, speaking to a crowd. Because of the tatters in the papyrus, the effect of trying to read it is like being present but being too far back to hear well. This must have happened often enough. "Blessed are the *who*? Did he say the swineherd was *welcomed* home?" Yeshua says something about a dark and secret place, and about weighing things that are weightless. That sounds like him. But then we are told that he threw a handful of seeds into the Jordan and that they became trees bearing fruit in the twinkling of an eye, and floated away down the river.

This, too, is familiar in its unfamiliarity. If he could wither a tree, he could create one. If he could walk on water, he could make an orchard stand on it. If this gospel had been known before 1935, what wonderful paintings the Renaissance would have made of it— a Botticelli is easy to imagine. We also recognize the mythic accretion that had begun before the gospels were written. Yeshua probably built a metaphor around the mystery of germination. In the retelling, and retelling, the metaphor transmuted into a magician's illusion.

His hearers understood hyperbole and parables as if by second nature. Faith should be so strong that it can move a mountain. Only a child would take that literally, and he kept asking us to become the kind of child who could believe it. He was remembered with this same kind of hyperbole that was native to the Hebraic imagination: They said he could magically multiply fish and bread (to praise his generosity), that he could walk on water, make the blind see and the dead come alive.

He wrote nothing. It is as if Heraclitus had not written a book but told his philosophy to grocers, fish-sellers, and housewives. True, like Socrates, who wrote nothing either, he was surrounded by disciples who understood that they were to carry on.

What they, or somebody, remembered were his sayings. When the gospels were written and by whom we do not know. "Matthew," "Mark," "Luke," and "John" are probably fictitious names. Yeshua's life was already a myth (which can coincide with truth and be a more vivid and symmetrical presentation of truth). History, in a *coup de théâtre* worthy of Beckett, swept away practically all traces of the historical Yeshua. Our certainties are three: He joined as a man in his thirties a reform movement led by one Yohannan, called "the Dipper" as he had revived an ancient ritual of symbolically washing away sin by immersion in running water. He had a coherent and charismatic ethic that he preached along roads and in the open country for three years. He fell into the hands of the Roman colonial authorities, who reluctantly respected the charge against him that he was a revolutionary and disruptive presence. He was cruelly executed by being nailed alive to an upright stake with a crosspiece for the hands. Such a mode of execution is torture, not dispatch.

In the logia, we see only the eloquent, wry, amused, and angry Yeshua; or, rather, we hear him. The falsest myth about him may be the Romantic and Sunday school pictures of him as a pious matinee idol with a woman's hair, neat beard, and flowing robes. History *can* tell us that he wore trousers of the kind we call Turkish, that he most certainly had oiled sidelocks and a full beard. A man so out-of-doors would have worn a wide-brimmed traveler's hat, a caftan, or coat. His sandals are mentioned by Yohannan. We can guess a witty smile

("Behold an Hebrew in whom is no guile!") and eyes capable of extreme sternness and kindness. That he could hold an audience entranced goes without saying.

Yeshua was the real ironist Kierkegaard conceals behind the face of Socrates in his doctoral thesis. Irony was his constant mode; it awakens the reflective faculties. A father loves his wayward better than his obedient son. Finding lost things pleases us more than knowing where they are. Adhering strictly to the law is strangely to disobey it. Riches are worth nothing. Heaven is not up but inside. His ironic paradoxes and his often mystifying parables replicate the strategies of Diogenes centuries before.

His paradox that stung worst was that religion anaesthetizes religion. Any two people, loving and agreeing with each other, was church enough, as it had been for Amos seven hundred years earlier. Identities aroused Swiftian satire in him, for "the kingdom of heaven" recognizes no identity but *human*. The only titles it uses are mother, father, daughter, son. Being—the vast universe of stars, the deserts of Edom, the animals and plants— is contained in Yeshua's word *father*, the progenitor of everything. This is a lot of family, yet Yeshua imagined this procreator as being so solicitous that he counts dead sparrows and knows the number of hairs on our heads. With Heraclitus he understood that Being is all of one substance, one origin, and one fate. We are all the prodigal children of one father.

In the logia we can scarcely discern the metaphysics and eschatology that the church, beginning with Paul, built around the vision Yeshua had of a redeemed humanity. The great stumbling block for the rational mind is, of course, belief. Believe—believe *what?*—and be saved; doubt and be damned. If Yeshua's death was a sacrifice to save us, we are saved, Hindus and pagans alike, senators, drug dealers, Irish Catholics, and TV evangelists. Lifeboats around a sinking ship do not sell tickets.

These logia are not everything that Yeshua said. Dialogue and narrative statements—even those as dramatic as "I have seen Satan falling like lightning from the sky"—are not logia. A logion is aphoristic, self-contained, and infinitely quotable.

The Dutch theologian Edward Schillebeeckx sees the Yeshua of our logia as a chrysalis stage of what he became after the first Easter. He is still *Jesus*. His transformation into *ho christos*, "the anointed," and his identification by Christians as the messiah happened after his time on earth. We can even read the Greek for "dwell among us" as "dwell *in* us." The preposition allows of either reading. Schillebeeckx also thinks that all presentations of Jesus in art and literature—in "the round of fiddles" Bach uses for his voice in his *St. Matthew Passion*, the Jesus of Dostoevsky and Kazantzakis, of Tolstoy and Balzac—should be seen as witnesses to his tragic vision of mankind as a community capable of compassion, love, and cooperation.

"The New Testament is a wonderful book," Thoreau said. "It should be read in churches on Sundays."

GUY DAVENPORT

The Logia of Yeshua

The Sayings of Jesus

1

If you haven't understood the *alef*, how can you teach others the *beth*?

2

[To his mother and brothers who wanted him, along with them, to be immersed by Yohannan for the remission of sins] In what have I sinned that I need to be immersed by him? Unless, of course, this very thing I'm saying is a sin of ignorance and presumption.

3

Come with me and I'll show you how to fish for people.

4

You that are destitute, rejoice: our father's
      kingdom shall be yours.
Rejoice, you that are hungry: you shall feast.
You that weep: you shall laugh with joy.
Rejoice, you that are persecuted: our father
      knows you and you will know him.

5

If our father's country were the sky, birds
would belong there more than you. If it were
the sea, the fish. But our father's realm is inside
you! You will understand this when you know
yourselves for what you are, the children of the
creator of all living things.

6

The kingdom of our father is like a mustard
seed, the smallest of all seeds, but when it falls
on ready ground it grows to be a large plant
and a shelter for the birds of the sky. Our

father's country is like the yeast which a wife hides down in fifty pounds of flour until it all rises. Our father's country is like a buried treasure turned up by a plow in the field: the farmer who finds it sells all that he owns to buy that field. Our father's country is like a perfectly round pearl: the merchant who sees it sells all his goods to buy it.

A man went out with a handful of seeds and scattered them. Some fell on the road and the birds ate them. Some fell on rocks and withered when they came up. Some fell among thorns and were choked. Some fell on good ground: they yielded thirty-fold, sixty-fold, a hundred-and twenty-fold. Our father's country is like the sowing of seeds: the man who sows them goes to sleep every night. He rises every day, and all the while the seeds sprout and grow, without his knowing how they do it. Oh yes! the earth knows how to bear fruit—first a little shoot, then the head, and at the last the ripe grain of wheat. And when it is ready for harvesting, the sickle brings it down into a heap.

A woman lost a silver coin, and when she found it, she valued it above all the rest of her money. A shepherd had a hundred sheep, and one of them got lost. He left the ninety-nine to look for it, and that stray, when he found it, was sweeter to him than the ninety-nine who had stayed together.

There was a rich man with a manager of his estate against whom charges were brought that he was wasting his boss's property. *What's this I hear?* the rich man said. *Let me see your accounts, as you no longer work for me.*

The manager thought: What am I going to do? I can't dig ditches, and I'm too proud to beg. But ah! I know what to do that people will respect me. He called his boss's debtors in, one by one. *How much do you owe my boss?* he asked the first.

Ten thousand liters of olive oil.

Here's your bill, the manager said. *Sit down and change the amount to one thousand.*

To another he said: *How much do you owe?*

A thousand bushels of wheat.

Take your bill, the manager said, *and change it to eight hundred.*

The rich man praised this dishonest manager for his shrewdness.

7

The owner of a vineyard went out at dawn to hire workers. He settled with some laborers for a dinar a day, and sent them out to the vineyard. He went out again three hours later and saw other workers idle in the marketplace. He told them, *Go out to my vineyard and whatever seems right I will pay you.* So they went. Going out again at noon and at three hours after noon, he did the same thing. Now about an hour before sunset he went out and found others who were loitering.

Why do you stand around idle all day? he asked them.

Nobody, they said, *has hired us.*

Go to my vineyard, he said.

And when evening came, the owner of the vineyard said to his manager, *Call the workers and pay them their wages, beginning with the last, up to the first.*

When those hired at the last hour came, they each received a dinar. When those hired first came, they thought they would get something more. But they each got a dinar, too. They took it and grumbled. *Those last guys only worked for one lousy hour, but you have paid them the same as us who did most of the work and in the hottest part of the day.*

To which the manager replied, *Friend, I've done you no wrong. You agreed, didn't you, to work for a dinar? Is there any law against my doing what I want to with my money? Are you not speaking out of envy?*

8

A man had two sons. To the first he said one day, *Son, go and work in the vineyard.* This son said *Yes,sir,* but never went.

The father sent his other son to work in the vineyard, too, but his reply was *I don't want to.* But later he thought better of it and went. Which of the two did what his father wanted?

9

There was a good man who had a vineyard. He leased it to tenant farmers to work it, but he was going to keep the crop for himself. When he sent a servant to collect the rent, they grabbed him, beat him, and well nigh killed him. He returned to tell the boss. They didn't recognize him, the boss thought. So he sent another servant, and the tenants beat him up, too.

So the boss sent his own son, thinking, Perhaps they will respect my son. But because the tenants knew him to be the heir to the vineyard, they killed him.

As it is written: the stone that the builders rejected has become the cornerstone (this is in the 118TH psalm, verse 22).

10

A king wished to settle all his accounts with his servants. When the accounting began, one was brought to him who owed him six million dinars. As he could not pay, the king ordered him and all his goods to be sold so that payment could be made. The servant fell on his face before him, begging, *Have patience with me, and I will pay you back everything!* Being merciful, the king dismissed him and forgave the debt.

But that same servant, as he went out, met a fellow servant who owed him a hundred dinars. Collaring him, he demanded, *Pay me what you owe me!*

The fellow servant fell on his face before

him, begging, *Have patience with me, and I will pay you back everything!* He refused and had him sent to debtor's prison.

When the other servants heard of this, they were distressed and went to tell the king what had happened. The king sent for the servant. *You evil wretch of a slave!* he shouted. *I forgave you your debt because you begged me to. Shouldn't you have had for your fellow slave the same pity I had for you?* In anger he turned him over to the bailiffs.

11

How can you say, I have kept the law and the prophets, when it is written in the law: You shall love your neighbor as yourself? And look, many sons of Abraham, your brothers, are clothed in filth and dying of hunger, while your house is full of good things, none of which goes to them.

12

It is easier for a camel to go through the eye of a needle than for a rich man to enter the kingdom of heaven.

13

A king, planning a banquet for his son's wedding, sent his servants out to invite guests to it. But one said, *I have financial claims on some merchants who are coming to see me this evening. I must go and give them orders, and ask to be excused from the banquet.*

Another said, *I have just bought a house, and people need me for the day. I'll have no time.*

Another said, *I have just bought a village and am on my way to collect the rents. I ask to be excused.*

So the bridegroom said, *Go into the streets and alleys and bring back the destitute, the crippled, the blind, and the lame to our banquet. There will be no merchants in my father's palace.*

14

What did you go out into the desert to see, a reed shaking in the wind? Really, what did you go to see? A man in fine clothes? Look, the elegantly dressed are in royal palaces, and they are ignorant of the truth. Among all those born of woman, none is greater than Yohannan the Dipper. But, I say again, whoever among you becomes a child will recognize our father's kingdom and be greater than Yohannan.

15

Yohannan fasted, and they said he was possessed by a devil. I eat and drink, and they say I am a glutton and a drunkard. They are like children playing in the market, chanting:

> We piped to you, and you didn't dance!
> We played a dirge, and you didn't cry!

16

A son and daughter shall inherit together. [To a woman in the crowd, who replied to this, *The womb is blessed that gave you birth, and the breasts that gave you milk*] Blessed are those who hear the word of the father and truly keep it. It will be said in days to come that the wombs are happy that have never given birth, and breasts that have never given milk.

17

Let anyone who has power renounce it.

18

I have lit a fire on the earth and shall watch over it until it blazes. Whoever is near me is near the fire, and whoever is far from me is far from the kingdom of our father.

19

Foxes have dens, and birds have nests, but the son of man has no place to rest his head.

20

Why do you wash the outside of the cup? Don't you understand that the maker of the outside also made the inside?

21

Come to me. You will find rest. My yoke is comfortable.

22

You see a cloud rising in the west and say, *It's going to rain.* When the wind blows from the south you say, *It's going to be a scorcher.* So why don't you know how to interpret the times now?

23

Seek, and you will find. Knock, and the door will be opened.

24

Who of you would give his son a rock when he asks you for bread? Who would give him a snake when he asks for a fish? If you, shiftless as you are, know how to give good things to your children, how much more will our father in heaven know what to give you.

25

Don't give sacred things to dogs, or throw pearls to pigs. They will trample them underfoot, or turn and tear you to shreds.

26

If you have money to lend, take no interest. Give it to someone from whom you won't get it back.

27

Those who obey my father are my mother and my brothers and my sisters.

28

[Upon being asked if it is lawful to pay Roman taxes] Show me a dinar. Whose face and epigraph are on it? Pay Caesar what is Caesar's; God what is God's.

29

Our father's kingdom is not going to come with people watching for it. No one is going to be able to say, *Look, here!* or, *Over there!* For the kingdom is inside you, waiting for you to find it.

30

The last will be first, and the first will be last.

31

There is nothing hidden that will not be revealed.

32

When people welcome you, heal the sick among them and eat whatever they set in front of you. Love your friends like your own soul. Protect them like the pupil of your eye.

33

You see a tiny sliver in your friend's eye, while not noticing the plank in your own! When you have cleared your own eye, then you can see to clear your friend's.

34

No prophet is welcome in his home town.

35

A city built on a high hill cannot be hidden.
No one lights the lamp and puts it under a
basket, but on a lampstand, so all coming and
going can see its light.

36

If a blind man leads a blind man, both of them
will stumble.

37

No one can rob a strong man's house without
first tying his hands.

38

Don't worry about what you're going to eat or
to wear. Our life is more than food, our bodies
more than clothing. Look at the birds: they
don't plant or harvest or gather into barns. Our
father feeds them, and aren't you more valuable

to him than birds? Can you lengthen your life by worrying? Look at the anemones: they don't card or spin, but the wives of Solomon in all their elegance had no dresses as beautiful. If our father dresses the fields with such color, will he not, O distrusting people, care even more for you? Whoever has a crust of bread in his basket and frets about tomorrow has little faith.

39

Be as watchful as snakes and as innocent as doves.

40

Whoever has will be given more, whoever has nothing, it will be taken away. This world is a bridge. Do not build your house on it. Be a traveler passing through.

41

Grapes do not grow on thorns or figs on this-
tles.

42

No one can work for two bosses. He will be
loyal to one and offend the other.

43

Who wants to drink a new rather than a vin-
tage wine?

44

If circumcision were useful, we would be born
without foreskins.

45

Our father's kingdom is like a man who sowed
good seed in his fields, but at night his enemy
came and sowed darnel weed. The fieldhands
asked, *Do you want us to pull up the weeds?*

No, the landowner said, *for you will pull up the wheat with it. Let them grow together until the harvest, when they will be easy to sort out.*

46

Do not let your right hand know what your left hand is doing.

47

There was a rich farmer with an abundant crop, and he thought to himself, *What shall I do? There's no room for storing all this produce.* It never occurred to him that he might share his abundance with the hungry and needy. Instead, he planned to pull down his barn and build a bigger one. And that very night he died.

48

[To a man who pleaded, *Rabbi, tell my brother to share the family inheritance with me*] Mister, who made me an arbiter in the division of property?

49

The sick, not the healthy, need a doctor.

50

Can the wedding guests fast while the bride-groom is with them?

51

Nobody pours fresh wine into old wineskins. If they did, the wineskins would burst and spill the wine. Fresh wine must go into new wineskins.

52

The *Shabbat* was made for people, not people for the *Shabbat*.

53

What goes into your mouth cannot defile you, but what comes out can.

54

What good is it to lose one's life in acquiring the world?

55

What would a person give in return for life?

56

Whoever wants to be first of all has to be last of all—and everybody's servant!

57

Anybody who is not against us is in favor of us.

58

If the saltiness goes out of salt, how can it be made salty again?

59

Whoever divorces his wife and marries another commits adultery.

60

Let the children come to me. Don't keep them
back. The country of our father belongs to
them.

61

Beware of scholars who like to wear fancy
clothes.

62

It is written in the scriptures: *You shall not murder.*
But I tell you, any who has a grudge against his
brother is in danger of our father's judgment,
and whoever says *Idiot!* to his brother shall
answer for it in his court, and whoever says *Fool!*
shall be in danger of the fires of Gehenna. So,
if in bringing your offering to the altar you
remember that your brother has a grudge
against you, leave your offering then and there
and go and be reconciled with your brother,
and then return to make your offering.

63

If you are on your way to court, come to a
friendly agreement with your opponent on
the way. The worst settlement out of court
is better than the best you can hope for from
the court. Once your case is before a judge,
chances are that he will hand you over to the
bailiff, who will lock you up until you have
paid the last penny.

64

Do not swear by the heavens, because they are
the throne of God. Do not swear by the earth,
as it is his footstool. Do not swear at all! Let
your yes be your yes, and your no your no.

65

Meet meanness with generosity, evil with good.
If a man slaps you on one cheek, turn so that

he can slap the other. If a man takes your shirt,
give him your coat as well. If you are made to
go a mile, go two.

66

Give to the beggar, lend to the borrower.

67

Love your enemy. Ask God to prosper those
who hurt you. Only then will you be a true
child of our father. Loving those who love you
needs no reward; even the unrighteous love.
What merit is there in being kind to those who
are kind to you? Your father is compassionate
to all, as you should be.

68

When you say your prayers, say: Father, may
your kingdom be ours. Give us bread for today.

Overlook our indebtedness to others, as we overlook theirs to us. Give us the strength to resist temptations.

69

Say your prayers in a room by yourself, and shut the door.

70

Make no hoard of earthly goods, which thieves can find and steal, and which moths can eat. Be rich, rather, in your spirit, which no thief can rob and no moth eat. For where your eye is, there is your heart.

71

When you fast, be cheerful. Wash your face and comb your hair.

72

Treat people the way you want them to treat you.

73

Aren't sparrows worth about a penny each? Yet not one of them dies without our father knowing it. As for you, even the hairs on your head have been counted. Fear not: you are worth more to him than sparrows.

74

Who accepts you accepts me, and who accepts me accepts who has sent me.

75

The law and the prophets ruled in Israel until Yohannan was slain. Violent men have taken the kingdom by force.

76

If your brother has done wrong and is sorry for it, take him into your company and forgive him seven times in a day. [And when Simeon asked, *Seven times in a day?*] Yes, and I will tell you, not only seven times but seven times seventy. Because even with the prophets, when the holy spirit was with them, yet a trace of sinfulness was still in them.

77

You have seen your brother, you have seen your God.

78

A pearl lost in mud is not less valuable. A pearl coated with balsam is not more valuable. We have our value from our father, and how and where we live cannot change it.

79

If you have a mustard seed of faith, and if two of you in peace together become as one, as I and my father are one, you can say to the mountain *Move away!* and it will.

A man leaving on a journey entrusted his property to his servants. To each of three servants in command he gave a thousand dinars. To others he gave lesser amounts, each according to his abilities. After a long while he returned and asked for an account from each servant. One came forward. *Boss,* he said, *you gave me a thousand dinars. I have traded with them and made five thousand more.* The man said, *Well done! You are a good and faithful servant. I will put you in charge of important matters.*

The second servant came forward and said, *Boss, I was afraid I would lose your money so I buried it where it would be safe. Here it is.*

Lazy servant! said the boss. *You could at least have invested my money with the moneylenders so that I would have the capital and interest, too.* So he took the lazy servant's money and gave it to the industrious one.

Then he called the third servant, who was hiding in fear. The others said, *Boss, he has spent your money on whores and girls who dance to the flute in the wine shops, on fine dinners and the bottle. We got after him for it, but he said we didn't know when you would be coming home, and kicked us.*

And the man had him bound and thrown in prison, to cry and grind his teeth.

81

Look, it is written: Honor your father and your mother, that the days given you on earth by the Lord your God may be many.

Yet the Sadducees and the House of Shammai go against the word of God. They say that one who donates to the temple what he might have given his parents is no longer obliged to support his father or his mother. They try to negate the word of God with a false tradition. Well did Yeshayahu prophesy of them:

Because this people approaches me with its
    mouth,
And with its lips they honor me,
But their veneration of me is vanity:
Commandments of man is their teaching!

Woe unto you, O House of Shammai! You
collect tithes from the leaves, pods, and stalks
of mint, anise, and cumin, and pass over what's
important in the Torah—justice, mercy, and
the love of God.

Woe unto you, O House of Shammai! You
clean the outside of the cup only. Inside yourselves there's extortion, rapacity, wickedness.

Woe unto you who build the tombs of the
prophets, who decorate the monuments of the
righteous! You consent to the actions of your
fathers: they killed the prophets and you build
the tombs.

82

They choke on a gnat and swallow a camel.

83

There was a man who had two sons. The younger one said to him, *Father, give me my share of the property now.* So the man divided his property between his two sons. After a few days the younger son sold his part of the property and left home with the money. He went to a country far away, where he wasted his life in reckless living, and spent all his money, and was left without a penny. So he went to a work for a man in that country, who sent him out to his farm to keep his pigs. How he wished he could fill his belly like the pigs with their carobs!

Thus at last he came to his senses, thinking how his father's hired hands had more to eat than he, who was starving. *I'll go back and say, Father, I have sinned against heaven and against you. I*

*don't deserve to be called your son. Treat me as one of
your hired hands.*

So he went back home. While he was still a
long way off, his father saw him and was filled
with pity. He ran to meet him, threw his arms
around him, and kissed him. The son started
to say, *Father, I have sinned against heaven and against
you. I don't deserve to be called your son,* but his father
called to the servants, *Make haste! Bring my best
robe and put it on him. Let us have a banquet and rejoice.
My son was dead, and he has come back to life!*

The elder son, who had been working in the
fields, heard as he was returning the musicians
playing dances. He called a boy to ask what
was going on. *Your brother has come home, and your
father has ordered a banquet to celebrate his return safe
and sound.*

The elder son was angry and refused to
attend. His father pleaded with him, but he
replied, *Look, I've served you as faithfully as a slave all*

my life. I've never disobeyed any word of yours. Now
your son who squandered your property on whores has
come home, has he? And you honor him with a banquet!

The father said, *My son, you're always with me.
All I have is yours. But your brother was dead and has
returned to life.*

84

By their fruits will you know them.

85

It is true what I tell you: if a seed does not fall
to the ground and die, it is nothing. But if it
dies, it is alive, takes root, and grows, bearing
fruit and seed in turn.

86

Don't judge if you don't want to be judged.
The measure you use for others will be used on
you.

87

The light of the body is the eye. When your eye is flawless, your whole body is full of light. But if your eye is imperfect, your whole body will be full of darkness.

88

Who promotes himself will be demoted, who demotes himself, promoted.

89

There was a judge who did not venerate God and did not care about people. There was a widow who kept coming to him, pleading for a ruling to protect her from an enemy. For the longest time he was unwilling, but eventually he thought, *Even though I'm not afraid of God and couldn't care less about people and their troubles, this widow has made a pest of herself. I must see that she gets justice before she wears me out.*

90

Who would save his life will lose it, who loses
his life will save it.

91

Two men went to the temple to pray. One was
a scholar of the law, the other a tax collector.
The scholar stood proudly and prayed about
himself, *I thank you that I'm not a robber, an adulterer,
or a tax collector. I keep all the commandments, I fast
twice a week, I pay tithes on all I earn.*

The tax collector stood apart and dared not
even raise his eyes. He beat his chest, saying, *O
God, be merciful to me, a sinner!*

I tell you, this man, and not the other, left
the temple upright in the sight of the father.

92

There was a rich man, so rich that he wore
purple like a king, and ate like one every day.

Meanwhile, a poor man named Eleazar sat miserably at his door, covered with sores and longing to eat the crumbs from the floor under the rich man's table. Dogs came to lick his sores.

This poor man died and was taken to heaven to feast with Avraham. The rich man, in time, died too, was buried, and went to his torments in Sheol. He could, by raising his eyes, see Avraham in heaven, with Eleazar at his side. *Father Avraham!* he called, *have mercy on me! Have Eleazar dip the tip of his finger in water to cool my tongue, to lessen that little bit the pain of this fire!*

But Avraham answered, *Remember, my child, your life was rich in blessings, while Eleazar had none at all. He has his reward and you have yours. Because you had no mercy on him, there is no way he can be merciful to you across the great chasm between us.*

93

Ask for the great things, and the small things
shall be yours as well.

Ask for the heavenly things, and the earthly
things shall be yours as well.

94

A man had a fig tree planted in his vineyard,
and he came looking for figs but found none.
So he said to his vinekeeper, *Look, three years I've
expected figs from this tree and there are none. Cut it
down. It takes up space.*

But the vinekeeper said, *Please let it stand, sir,
just one more year, and let me trench around it and put
on manure. If it bears fruit next year, well and good. If
not, I'll cut it down.*

95

[Entering the temple, ordering the merchants
to leave, folding up the tables of the moneylenders, driving out the sellers of doves, sheep,

and oxen] Take all these things away! It is written in the book of the prophet Yeshayahu, My house shall be called a house of prayer for all the nations. And it was prophesied through Yirmiahu, Has this house, which is called by my name, become a cave for robbers? And the father has spoken through Zekhariah: There shall be no more merchants in the house of the Lord of Hosts in that day.

96

[Sitting opposite the treasury of the temple, watching the rich give large amounts and a poor widow two small copper coins] This poor widow has given more than all the rest, for she gave all she had.

97

The first of the commandments is: Hear, O Israel, the Lord is our God, the Lord is one. And you are to love the Lord your God with all your heart, with all your being, with all your understanding, and with all your strength. The second is, You are to love your neighbor as yourself. There is no other commandment greater than these.

98

A traveler was going from Yerushalayim to Yerikho when highwaymen attacked him, stripped him, beat him, and left him half dead. Now it happened that a priest was traveling on that same road. Seeing the wounded man, he passed by on the other side. A Levite, also, came along, looked at him, and passed by on the other side. But a Palestinian, coming along next, was moved to pity. He bandaged his wounds after pouring oil and wine on them. He set him on his donkey and took him to an inn and arranged with the innkeeper for him to be taken care of. Next day, he left two dinars

for his keep, promising on his return journey
to pay more if needed.

And which of these three was a good neighbor?

99
It is better to give than to be given to.

100
Suppose one of you has a friend who comes at
midnight saying, *Friend, lend me three loaves of bread!
A friend of mine who is traveling has just arrived and I
have nothing to give him!*

Suppose you reply, *Don't bother me! My door's
bolted for the night; my kids and I are in bed.*

I tell you, even if you won't get up and give
him bread because he's your friend, because of
his *khutspah* you'll rouse yourself and give him
as much as he needs.

When the king comes in his glory, and all the heavenly messengers with him, then he will sit on his throne, with all the nations gathered before him, and he will separate them into two groups, at his right hand and at his left, just as a shepherd separates the sheep from the goats.

The king will say to those on his right hand, *You, having the father's blessing, inherit the kingdom that was prepared for you since the creation of the world. I was hungry and you fed me, I was thirsty and you gave me drink. I was a stranger and you welcomed me in your house. I was naked and you gave me clothes. I was sick and you visited me. I was in prison and you came to me.*

The righteous will say, *Lord, when did we see you hungry and feed you, or thirsty and gave you drink? When did we welcome you as a stranger, or clothe your nakedness? And when did we visit you sick or in prison?*

The king will answer, *What you did to the least of my brothers and sisters you did to me.*

Then he will say to those at his left hand, *Go away from me, for you are lost, into the eternal fire prepared for the devil and his messengers, because I was hungry and you did not care, because I was thirsty and you did not care. I was a stranger and you turned me away, I was naked and you gave me no clothes, I was sick and in prison and you kept your distance.*

They will answer, *Lord, when did we see you hungry or thirsty or a stranger or naked or sick or in prison?* And he will answer them, *In all truth I tell you, when you failed in charity toward the humblest of my brothers and sisters, you failed in charity to me. It's not those who say, Lord, Lord! who will enter the father's kingdom, but those who do his will.*

102

[At the time for Passover, his disciples having asked him where they were to prepare the Passover lamb] Why do you think I want to

eat flesh just because it's the time of Passover?
[Taking bread, breaking it, blessing it, and giving it to his disciples] This is my body.

[Pouring wine into a cup and giving thanks]
This is my blood. It is a covenant poured for
you and for many. Take it. I will not taste wine
until our father's kingdom comes.

103

Yerushalayim! Yerushalayim! You that kill the
prophets and stone those sent to you! How
often, if you had let me, would I have gathered
your children as a hen her chicks under her
wings!

104

[Appearing to Yaakob, who had vowed he
would not eat from the hour he had drunk the
Lord's cup until he saw him risen from them
that sleep] Bring a table and bread. Eat, my
brother, for I am him who has risen from them
that sleep.

105

Look, I'm always with you, until the end of
time. Lift up a stone, you'll find me there; split
wood, I'm there.

Sources and Notes

Most of these logia are accepted as authentic by the scholarly consensus. A few logia, and portions of logia, are included even though they do not enjoy such wide scholarly support. For them, we have included longer notes, with our reasons for inclusion. We hope thereby to stimulate new avenues of scholarly debate.

1. Infancy Gospel of Thomas the Israelite (in M. R. James, *The Apocryphal New Testament*, where the translation is "Thou that knowest not the Alpha according to its nature, how canst thou teach others the Beta?"). Apodictic ascription is impossible, but this retort of the schoolboy Yeshua to his teacher Zacchaeus is remarkably consonant with his mature style.

    This Zacchaeus has been theorized to be Zakay, a Galilean teacher who was the father of Yohannan Bar Zakay, a famous first-century rabbi who was a contemporary of Yeshua. His father would certainly be of the right generation to be Yeshua's teacher. Both chronologically and geographically, the identification is plausible.

2.   Jerome, *Dialogue against Pelagius*, III:2, quoting "the
       Gospel according to the Hebrews, which is in truth
       in the Chaldean and Syrian [that is, Aramaic]
       speech but is written in Hebrew letters, which the
       Nazarenes use to this day, called 'according to the
       Apostles.' Or, as most term it, 'according to Mat-
       thew,' which is also to be seen in the library of
       Caesarea . . ."

       The "Nazarenes" (also called "Ebionites")
were the original Yeshua Movement. They were
Jewish people, including Yeshua's family and the
original apostles, who accepted Yeshua as Lord
and Messiah. Their gospel, derived largely from
family traditions of Mariam and her children, and
from personal recollections of Yeshua's closest
associates, deserves far more acceptance than it
generally receives.

       Many early Christians seem to have been em-
barrassed by the fact that Yeshua was baptized by
Yohannan. The Gospel of John neglects to mention this baptism (just as it forgets the kiss of
Judas and the tears of Peter, among many other
things). The Synoptics try several ploys. Yohannan
says *he* should be baptized by Yeshua, and not the
other way around. Misleading hints are given that
somebody else, not Yohannan, performed the Im-

mersion. Scholars in general (except for Robert Graves and Joshua Podro, who assert the priority of the Hebrew Gospel) take for granted that the story of Mariam and Yeshua's brothers persuading a reluctant Yeshua to go to Yohannan for Immersion belongs to the same category as the ploys of John and the Synoptics: an attempt to either deny the Immersion or at least to minimize the embarrassment of it. The former is untenable: we have plenty of evidence that the Hebrew Gospel included an account of the Immersion of Yeshua by Yohannan. Moreover, common sense plainly shows that this story would *add* to the embarrassment, not diminish it. The idea for this very important step in Yeshua's life does not even come from him, but from somebody else. Yeshua changes his mind. He admits he may be guilty of a sin after all. So plain common sense and logic outweigh the begging of the question by the majority of scholars.

And there is more. The Hebrew Gospel was produced by a community that included Yeshua's family. If this story had been invented by a non-member of the family, or even a maverick member, the family would have collectively and indignantly refuted it and prevented its inclusion in the gospel. It must have been an authentic family tradition.

3. Matthew 4:19, Mark 1:17, Luke 5:10. Against the unanimous testimony of all three synoptic gospels we have a scholarly contention that this logion reflects a concern of the church, not of Yeshua. We submit that Yeshua may have meant something different by it than what the church later interpreted it to mean.

4. Luke 6:20–21, Matthew 5:3–6, Thomas 54 and 69. The scholarly consensus is that the version in Luke is older and more authentic than that of Matthew. We agree with this, but we also insist that Thomas has wording in better harmony with Yeshua's most typical forms of speech when describing the *Basileia* as being "of the father" rather than "of God" or "of heaven." The latter is a circumlocution for "God"—but not an evasion that Yeshua found acceptable. See Luke 11:2, Matthew 6:9, etc.

   Destitute = Greek *ptokhoi* = Hebrew *evyonim* (the origin of the term *Ebionites*—see note to logion 2).

5. Luke 17:20–21, Thomas logia 3 and 113, Oxyrhyncus Papyrus 654:2, and some creative reconstruction by the two modern editors.

6. *Mustard seed.* Thomas 20:2–4, Mark 4:30–32, Luke 13:18–19, Matthew 13:31–32. Scholars consider the version in Thomas to be the most authentic.

The hidden yeast. Matthew 13:33, Luke 13:20, Thomas 96:1−2 (see also Genesis 18:6).

The treasure and the pearl. Matthew 13:44−46, Thomas 109:1−3 and 76:1−2.

Sowing and reaping. Matthew 13:1−9, Mark 4:1−9 and 26−29, Luke 8: 11−15.

Lost coin. Luke 15:8−9.

Lost sheep. Luke 15:4−6, Matthew 18:12−13, Thomas 107:1−3.

The shrewd manager. Luke 16:1−8.

7. Matthew 20:1−15.

8. Matthew 21:28−31.

9. Thomas, logia 65 and 66, Mark 12:1−11, Matthew 21:33−43, Luke 20: 9−18. In all four, Psalm 118:22 is quoted at the end. Such unanimous testimony (very rare in logia matters) is very strong evidence indeed that the verse was the story's coda from the very beginning.

10. Matthew 18:23−34.

11. The version of Matthew 19:16−24 found in the Gospel according to the Hebrews as quoted by Origen in his *Latin Commentary on Matthew 15:14*.

12. Matthew 19:24, Mark 10:25, Luke 18:25.

13. Thomas 64, Luke 14:16−24, Matthew 22:2−10. See also logion 95 and its notes.

14. Matthew 11:7–11, Luke 7:24–23, Thomas 78. See also logion 60 and its notes.

15. Matthew 11:16–19, Luke 7:31–35. Here and almost everywhere we translate "Son of Man" as simply "I," in accordance with Geza Vermes's conclusive demonstration that in Yeshua's authentic sayings it is a too-literal translation of the Aramaic *barnasha* ("this person"), a politely humble way of referring to oneself.

16. Talmud, *Tractate Shabbath* 116A–B, quoting from "the Gospel." Luke 11:27–25 and 23:29. Thomas 79.

17. Thomas 81, Dialogue of the Savior 20C.

18. *I have lit a fire on the Earth, / And shall watch over it until it blazes.* Jesus said, "I have cast fire upon the world, and look, I'm guarding it until it blazes." (Thomas 10) "I came to set the Earth on fire, and how I wish it were already ablaze!" (Luke 12:49)

    The authenticity of the logion is upheld by its independent attestation in both Thomas and Luke. The above is our best guess as to its original form. We have followed to some degree the scholarly consensus that the version in Thomas is closer than Luke's to the ur-form.

    The second half of logion 18 is found only in Thomas, and its authenticity is less certain. See also logion 105 and its notes.

19. Luke 9:58, Matthew 8:20, Thomas 86:1–2. See notes to logion 15.

20. Thomas 89:1–2, Matthew 23:25–26, Luke 11:39–41.

21. Matthew 11:28–30, Thomas 90.

22. Luke 12:54–56.

23. *Seek, and you will find; / Knock, and it will be opened. / One who seeks will find, / And for one who knocks it will be opened.* "Ask—it will be given to you. / Seek—you will find. / Knock—it'll be opened to you. / Be assured, / Everyone who asks receives, / Everyone who seeks, finds; / And for one who knocks it is opened." (Matthew 7:7–8; Luke 11:9–10) Jesus said, "Those who seek should not stop seeking until they find." (Thomas 2:1) Jesus said, "Seek and you will find." (Thomas 92:1) Jesus said, "One who seeks will find, and for one who knocks it will be opened." (Thomas 94:1–2)

Perhaps Matthew and Luke both copied this saying verbatim from Q (if the hypothetical Q gospel existed, which is not apodictical) or else Luke copied it verbatim from Matthew, or Matthew from Luke. Whichever theory is correct, the passages in Matthew and Luke do not really constitute two independent testimonies, but must be counted as one attestation.

Thomas provides close parallels for the second and third elements of the Matthean-Lukan formulation, but not the first. Yeshua, being Jewish, liked to express himself in binary parallelism. I theorize here that Gentile editors, unfamiliar with Semitic poetic forms, had a tendency to expand Yeshua's couplets into triplets. I propose these as rules for determining the authenticity and original form of some logia of Yeshua. I do not expect them to be of universal application, but they may be useful in many cases.

24. Matthew 7:9–11, Luke 11:11–13.

25. Matthew 7:6, Thomas 93, Didache 9:5B.

26. Matthew 5:42, Luke 6:30.

27. Matthew 12:48–50, Thomas 99, Luke 8:21, Mark 3:33–35. The logion is probably authentic, but the story that frames it is probably an invention of elements within the early church that wanted to discredit Yeshua's family, who were the leaders of the Yeshua Movement, composed at first entirely of Messianic Jews.

28. Matthew 22:20, Mark 12:16, Luke 20:24, Thomas 100. See also Genesis 1:26–27.

29. Luke 17:20–21.

30. *The last will be first, / And the first will be last.* Matthew 20:16, Luke 13:30.

Matthew 19:30, Mark 10:31, and Thomas 4:2 have a qualified form: "Many of the first will be last." The qualified forms outnumber the unqualified three to two for the first half of the couplet, while for the second half they are equally balanced. However, the Fellows of the Jesus Seminar "are of the opinion that the unqualified form is more likely to have originated with Jesus, since his style is given to exaggeration, hyperbole, and overstatement. Furthermore, the first version . . . is more concise" and Yeshua preferred conciseness. I find these arguments unimpeachable.

31. Matthew 10:26–27, Luke 12:2–3, Thomas 5:2 and 6:3.

32A. *When people welcome you, heal the sick among them and eat whatever they set in front of you.* Logion reconstructed from "Whenever you enter a town and they welcome you, eat whatever is set before you. Cure the sick there . . . " (Luke 10:8–9A) and "When you go into any region and walk about in the countryside, when people take you in, eat what they serve you, and heal the sick among them" (Thomas 14:4).

A majority of the scholars of the Jesus Seminar accepts the "eat whatever" injunction as probably coming from Yeshua; but they reject the "heal the sick" part. This is logically unacceptable. Luke and

Thomas give mutually supporting testimony that the two parts were linked together from the very beginning. Furthermore, healing the sick is an important and essential part of Yeshua's ministry.

Even though Professor John Dominic Crossan was one of the founders of the Jesus Seminar, he does not agree with its conclusion either, and includes the portion about healing in his version of this logion (number 17 in his compilation). Professor Crossan rightly points out that many of Yeshua's first envoys "must have been *healed healers* whose healing was not so much an instant event as a slow process in which mission was less a result than a part of the healing itself." Others, whose healing was faster and more dramatic, would consider it their duty in honor to show gratitude by healing others. Either way, the core of Yeshua's movement consisted then, and still consists, of missionaries whose mission is to teach and to heal. This they did, and do, by going from door to door and from town to town.

32B. *Love your friends like your own soul. Protect them like the pupil of your eye.* Thomas 25. (There is also an echo of this logion in John 13:34–35, but the version in Thomas is obviously more reliable than that of John.)

33. Matthew 7:5, Luke 6:41–42, Thomas 26:1–2.

34. Matthew 13:57, Mark 6:4, Luke 4:24, John 4:14, Thomas 31:1.

35A. Matthew 5:14, Thomas 32.

35B. Matthew 5:15, Mark 4:21, Luke 8:16 and 11:33, Thomas 33:2–3.

36. Matthew 15:14.

37. Matthew 12:29, Mark 3:27.

38A. Matthew 6:25–33, Luke 12:22–31.

The emendation from "Solomon" to "Solomon's wives" is by Robert Graves and Joshua Podro, who very convincingly aver that the original logion balanced in parallel the "male" activities of sowing and reaping with the "female" activities of carding and spinning. It is easy to see how the change must have been made by a church embarrassed by the hint of polygamy.

38B. Logion of Yeshua quoted by Rabbi Eliezer in Talmud Bavli (Babylonian Talmud), *Tractate Sota* 48B.

39. Matthew 10:16.

40A. *Whoever has something will be given more; / And whoever has nothing, it will be taken away.* Thomas 41:1–2, Mark 4:25, Matthew 13:L2, Luke 8:18. Each of the four has slight but significant differences from the other three. The above is only my best guess as to what the original form of the logion may have been.

40B. *This world is a bridge: Do not build your dwelling on it, but be passersby.* I have reconstructed this logion from two sources: (1) An Arabic inscription, 1601 A.D., on the southern gate of the city of Fatepuhr-Sikri, India, reads: "Jesus, on whom be peace, has said: 'This world is a bridge: Pass over it, but do not build your dwelling there.'" (2) Jesus said, "Be passersby." (Thomas 42)

The fact that the two attestations are so far apart in time—about fourteen centuries—and space (India, Egypt) certainly makes their mutual support all the more remarkable and strong. The claim that Thomas 42 has "no parallels" is an error.

Furthermore and undeniably, this logion is in perfect harmony with Yeshua's philosophy and way of life: Do not worry about tomorrow, do not store up treasures on Earth, etc.

41. Matthew 7:16, Luke 6:43, Thomas 45.

42. Matthew 6:24, Luke 16:13, Thomas 47:2.

43. Luke 5:39.

44. *Circumcision.* Found only in the Gospel of Thomas; but the very fact that it is so heretical, shocking, and outrageous argues in favor of its authenticity.

45. Matthew 13:24–30.

46. Matthew 6:3, Thomas 62:2.

47. Luke 12:16–20, Thomas 63:1–6, *The Nazarene Gospel Restored* (Graves and Podro).

48. Luke 12:13–14.

49. Matthew 9:12, Mark 2:17, Luke 5:31, Gospel Fragment 1224.

50. Matthew 9:15, Mark 2:19, Luke 5:34, Thomas 104.

51. Matthew 9:17, Mark 2:22, Luke 5:37–38, Thomas 47:4.

52. Matthew 12:1–8, Mark 2:27, Luke 6:1–5, Talmud Bavli (Babylonian Talmud) *Yoma* 85B and elsewhere ("The shabbat was given to you, not you to the shabbat," "The shabbat was given to Israel, not Israel to the shabbat").

53. Matthew 15:10–11, Mark 7:14–15, Thomas 14:5.

54. Matthew 16:26.

55. Matthew 16:26.

56. Matthew 20:25–28, Mark 10:42–45, Luke 22:24–30.

57. Mark 9:38–40, Luke 9:49–50, Oxyrhynchus Papyrus 1224.

58. Matthew 5:13, Mark 9:50, Luke 14:34–35.

59. Matthew 5:32, Luke 16:18.

60. Matthew 18:2–4 and 19:13–15, Mark 9:36 and 10:13–16, Luke 9:47–48 and 18:15–17, Thomas 78.

61. Matthew 23:5–7, Mark 12:38–39, Luke 11:43 and 20:46.

62. Matthew 5:21–24 (quoting Exodus 20:13). Matthew 5:23 here follows the text of the Peshitta and

the Old Syriac, which fits the context better than the Greek, both logically and poetically.

63. Matthew 5:25—26.

64. Matthew 5:33—37.

65. Matthew 5:39—40, Luke 6:29.

66. Matthew 5:42, Luke 6:30.

67. Matthew 5:44—48, Luke 6:32—36.

68. Matthew 6:9—13, Luke 11:2—4.

69. Matthew 6:1—8.

70. Matthew 6:20—21, Luke 12:33—34.

71. Matthew 6:16—18.

72. Matthew 7:12, Luke 6:31.

73. Matthew 10:29—31, Luke 12:6—7.

74. Matthew 10:40, Luke 10:16, John 13:20.

75A. Luke 16:16, Matthew 11:13.

75B. Matthew 11:12.

76. Matthew 18:21—22, Luke 17:4, The Gospel according to the Hebrews as quoted by Jerome in *Against Pelagius*, III:2.

77. Recorded both by Clement of Alexandria (*Miscellanea* 1:19: 94,5) and Tertullian (*On Prayer*, 26).

78. The Gospel according to Phillip, 41.

79. Matthew 13:31—32, Mark 4:30—32, Luke 13:18—19, Thomas 20:2—4.

80. Matthew 25:14—30 and Luke 19:12—27, 42—46,

12:45–46, and the description of the parable by Eusebius in his *Theophany*.

81A. Exodus 20:12.

81B. Matthew 15:8, Mark 7:6–13, Talmud: *Shabbat* 127B, *Arakhin* 28A, *Nazir* 9A. Harvey Falk, *Jesus the Pharisee*, pp. 96–99, Hyam Maccoby, *Revolution in Judea*.

81C. Isaiah 29:13.

81D. Matthew 23:23, Luke 11:42, the pronouncements of Rabbi Eliezer ben Hyrkanus (chief spokesman for the House of Shammai) in *Ma'asrot* (Tithes) 4:5,6.

81E. Matthew 23:25, Luke 11:39, Mishnah, *Tractate Brakhot* (Blessings) 52:A–B.

81F. Matthew 23:29–31, Luke 20:47–48.

82. Matthew 23:24.

83. Luke 15:11–32.

84. Matthew 7:16, Luke 6:44, Thomas 45:1.

85. John 12:24.

86. Matthew 7:2, Luke 6:37, I Clement 13:2.

87. Matthew 6:22–23, Luke 11:34.

88. Luke 14:11 and 18:14.

89. Luke 18:2–8, with emendations suggested by Joseph Fitzmyer, "The Gospel according to Luke" (Anchor Bible 28A), pp. 1175–81.

90. Matthew 16:25, Mark 8:35, Luke 9:24, John 12:25.

91. Luke 18:10–14, with emendations suggested by Jo-

seph Fitzmyer, op. cit., pp. 1183–89, Graves and Podro in *The Nazarene Gospel Restored*, and the Curetonian Syriac text.

92. Luke 16:19–26.

93. Origen, *On Prayer* 2,2; 14,1, Clement of Alexandria, *Miscellanea* I.24.158.

94. Luke 13:6–9.

95. Matthew 21:12–13, Mark 11:15–17, Luke 19:45–47, Isaiah 56:7, Jeremiah 7:11, Zachariah 14:21.

96. Mark 12:41–44, Luke 21:1–4.

97. Matthew 22:35–40, Mark 12:28–34.

98. Luke 10:29–37. *The Good Palestinian*: by now, "good Samaritan" is more of a redundancy than the oxymoron it was originally meant to be, thanks to centuries of hearing this parable. With this translation, we hope to restore the original shock. Besides, all Samaritans are Palestinians (though not all Palestinians are Samaritans). "A people occupying portions of the Holy Land in rivalry with the Jewish people" is as good a definition of first-century Samaritans as of twentieth-century Palestinians.

99. Acts 20:35.

100. Luke 11:5–8.

101. Matthew 25:31–45. "Son of man" in verse 31 is here emended to agree with "the King" in verses

34 and 40. Scholars are generally skeptical about this prophecy, on the grounds that Yeshua is not concerned with such apocalyptic themes in his authentic teaching. However, the apocalyptic setting is here only the medium, and the message is one of social responsibility and concern for others, themes that are undeniably central to Yeshua's ministry.

102A. The Ebionite Gospel according to Matthew, or Gospel according to the Hebrews, as quoted by Epiphanius in *Panarion* 30.22,4.

102B. Matthew 7:21 and 26:26, Mark 14:22, Luke 22:19, First Corinthians 11:25, Justin's *Apologia* I.66.3.

102C. Matthew 26:27–29, Mark 14:23–25.

103. Matthew 23:37–39, Luke 13:34–35. Matthew and Luke have identical wording, but place the logion in different times, places, and contexts.

104. The Gospel according to the Hebrews, quoted by Jerome in *On Illustrious Men*, 2.

105A. Matthew 28:20.

105B. Oxyrhynchus Papyrus One, logion 46.

These two logia, being two expressions of the same notion, support each other.

Elsewhere, Yeshua promises to be present in bread, in wine, in fire, and in the person of the poorest of the poor.

And, as Professor Davenport avers in his introduction, Yeshua is also present in art, in music, in literature. By one of those Jungian synchronicities, at the same time as this book was being prepared for publication, a new translation—reputed to be accurate, complete, detailed, and scholarly—of Mikhail Bulgakov's *The Master and Margarita* appeared. This great novel includes a story, "The Procurator of Judea," which is one of the three best literary representations of Yeshua that I have ever read. The other two are Philip José Farmer's short novel *Riverworld* (in some ways a sequel to Bulgakov's story), and of course Oscar Wilde's "The Selfish Giant."

BENJAMIN URRUTIA

About the Translators

GUY DAVENPORT is a poet, critic, and translator. He was born in South Carolina in 1927 and educated at Duke University, Merton College, Oxford, and Harvard University. He received an award for fiction from the American Academy and Institute of Arts and Letters in 1981 and was awarded a MacArthur Fellowship in 1992. In addition to his numerous books of fiction, essays, and poetry, Guy Davenport has published several volumes of translation, including, most recently, *Seven Greeks*. He lives in Lexington, Kentucky.

BENJAMIN URRUTIA is a teacher, linguist, and scholar who has been writing and publishing about the Bible for a quarter of a century. He was born in Guayaquil, Ecuador, and educated at Brigham Young University. His numerous articles on biblical subjects have appeared in *American Anthropologist*, *Dialogue*, *Egyptological Studies*, and *Mythlore*, among others. Benjamin Urrutia lives in Chicago.